CRITTERS FOR KIDS

A NORTH AMERICAN WILDLIFE ACTIVITY BOOK

Tom Hunter B. Ed.

Copyright © 1999 Tom Hunter

CANADIAN CATALOGUING IN PUBLICATION DATA

Hunter, Tom
  Critters for kids

    ISBN 1-895811-69-4

    1. Zoology—North America—-Juvenile literature. I. Title.
QL151.H86 1999 j591.97 C99-910696-1

First Edition 1999

Heritage House wishes to acknowledge the the Department of Canadian Heritage through the Book Publishing Industry Development Program, the Canada Council, and the British Columbia Arts Council for supporting various aspects of its publishing program. We also wish to acknowledge the valuable services provided by the British Columbia Archives and Records Service (BCARS) to enhance the visual presentation of this book.

Cover design: Tom Hunter
Cover layout: Darlene Nickull
Book layout: Cathy Mack and Jane Tobin

HERITAGE HOUSE PUBLISHING COMPANY LTD.
#108 - 17665 66 A Avenue, Surrey, B.C., V3S 2A7

Printed in Canada

The Gila monster lives in the Southwest, along with ten other desert dwellers that are hiding in the squares below. Look for them across or down.

R	B	R	A	T	J			
O	T	S	T	L	A		V	U
A	O	P	E	C	C	A	R	Y
D	R	S	N	A	K	E	M	S
R	T	A	P	F	R	X	O	K
U	O	Z	C	O	A	T	I	U
N	I	B	M	X	B	A	T	N
N	S	Y	W	F	B	G	L	K
E	E	C	E	D	I			
R	K	T	O	P	T	J		

The river otter's favorite food is fish. See if you can help it catch the trout by tracing a way through this maze with your pencil.

WHAT DO YOU KNOW ABOUT THE ROAD-RUNNER?

T   F

1. Road-runners are found in the extreme southern United States and Mexico. ☐ ☐

2. Road-runners usually lay four to six pale yellowish or chalky white eggs. ☐ ☐

3. The nest is usually found high up in ponderosa pine trees. ☐ ☐

4. The road-runner is a close relative of the cuckoo. ☐ ☐

5. Road-runners live almost entirely on small lizards. ☐ ☐

6. The road-runner often grows to be twelve to fifteen inches long. ☐ ☐

Answers:
1. True. 2. True. 3. False. The nest is found in thorny bushes and shrubs. 4. True. 5. True. 6. False. It is 20 to 24 inches long.

These little wild pigs of the Southwest have two names. To find out what these names are, over each letter write the letter that appears before it in the alphabet.

K B W F M J O B

Q F D D B S Z

DID YOU KNOW?

The tiny ant can lift and carry more than fifty times its own weight.

Try to draw this American buffalo or bison by copying one square at a time.

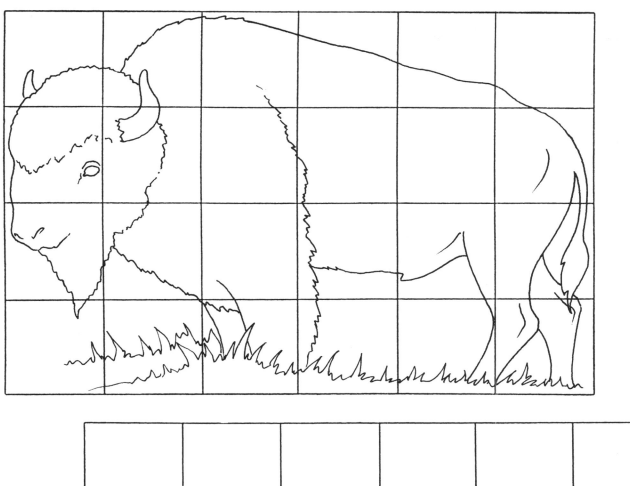

WHAT DO YOU KNOW ABOUT THE SCORPION?

TRUE OR FALSE

	T	F
1. Scorpions live on insects and spiders.	☐	☐
2. A scorpion's stinger is between its pincers.	☐	☐
3. Scorpions hunt their prey in daylight.	☐	☐
4. Scorpions are related to spiders.	☐	☐
5. Scorpions lay eggs in the sand.	☐	☐
6. Scorpions have been on earth 400 million years.	☐	☐

Answers: 1. True. 2. False. The stinger is on the end of the scorpion's tail. 3. False. The scorpion hunts only at night. 4. True. 5. False. Scorpions are born live. 6. True.

I am a seaperch. Below are six more seaperches. Which one do you think is exactly like me?

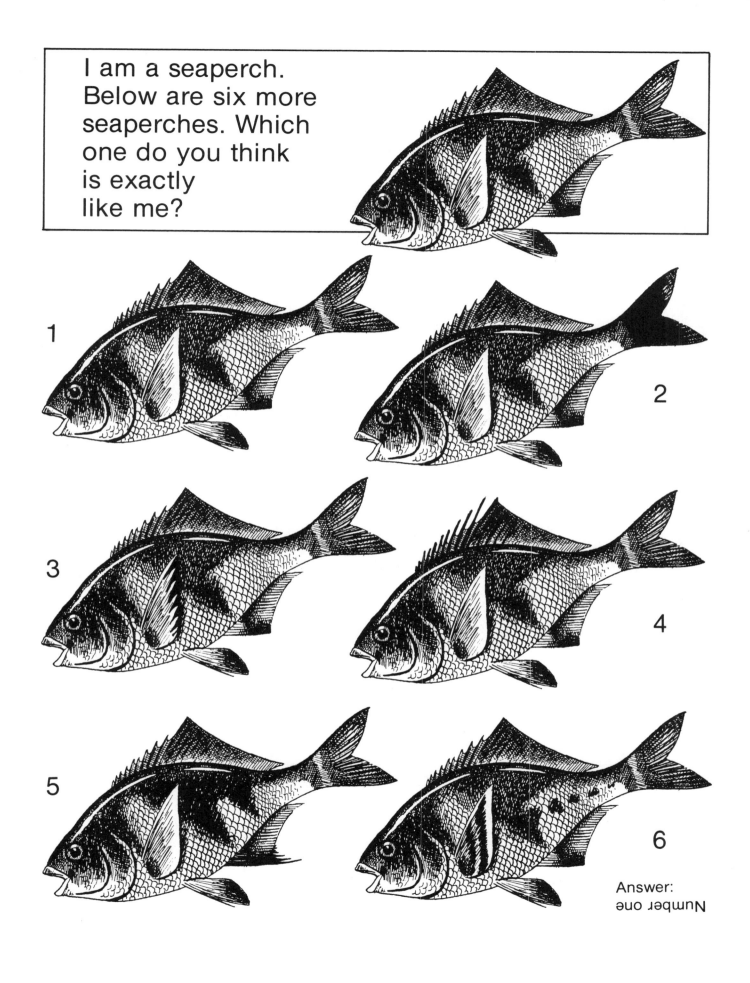

1

2

3

4

5

6

Have someone time you while you study the creatures on this page for one minute. Then close the book and write down the names of all the creatures you remember. Twelve would be good. Sixteen would be great!

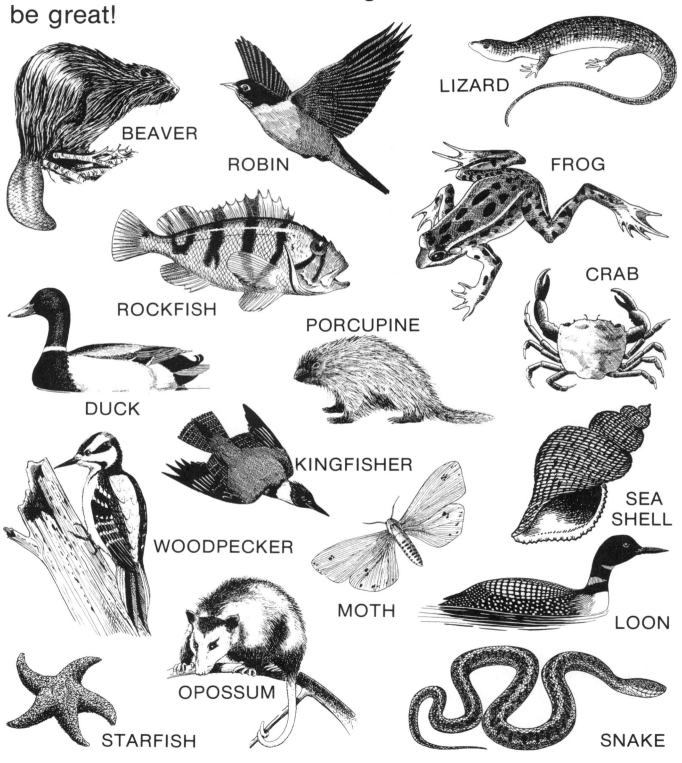

BEAVER

ROBIN

LIZARD

FROG

ROCKFISH

CRAB

PORCUPINE

DUCK

KINGFISHER

SEA SHELL

WOODPECKER

MOTH

LOON

STARFISH

OPOSSUM

SNAKE

This bird is a ruffed grouse.
See how many words you can
make from the letters in
the word "grouse."

GROUSE

_____   _____   _____

_____   _____   _____

_____   _____   _____

_____   _____   _____

_____   _____   _____

Hello there!
I'm a honey bee.
But just for today
I'm going to be a
spelling bee.
Test your skills
on the bird names
listed below.
Underline the
spelling you believe
to be correct.

roughed grouse	ruffed grouse
perigrine falcon	peregrine falcon
osprey	ospray
screach owl	screech owl
Arctic tern	Arctic turn
morning dove	mourning dove
ptarmigan	tarmigan
ringneck phesant	ringneck pheasant
killdeer	kildeer
cormorant	cormrant
mallerd	mallard

This scary creature can be found on both the Atlantic and Pacific coasts. It often grows longer than a hockey stick and has teeth like a dog. To find its name, over each letter below write the letter that appears after it in the alphabet.

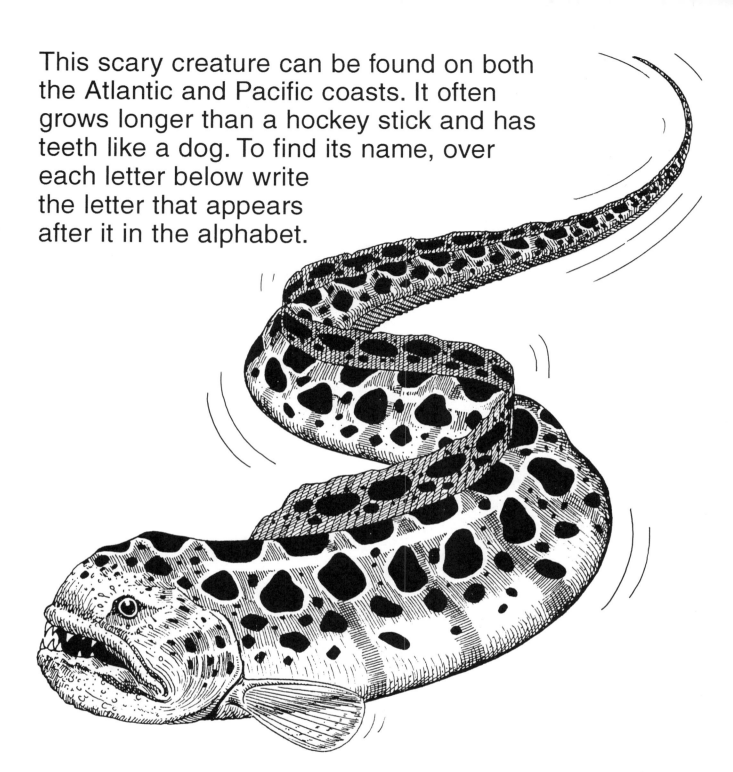

VNKE DDK

The praying mantis is one of 20 native species found in the South. Which shadow do you think belongs to this praying mantis?

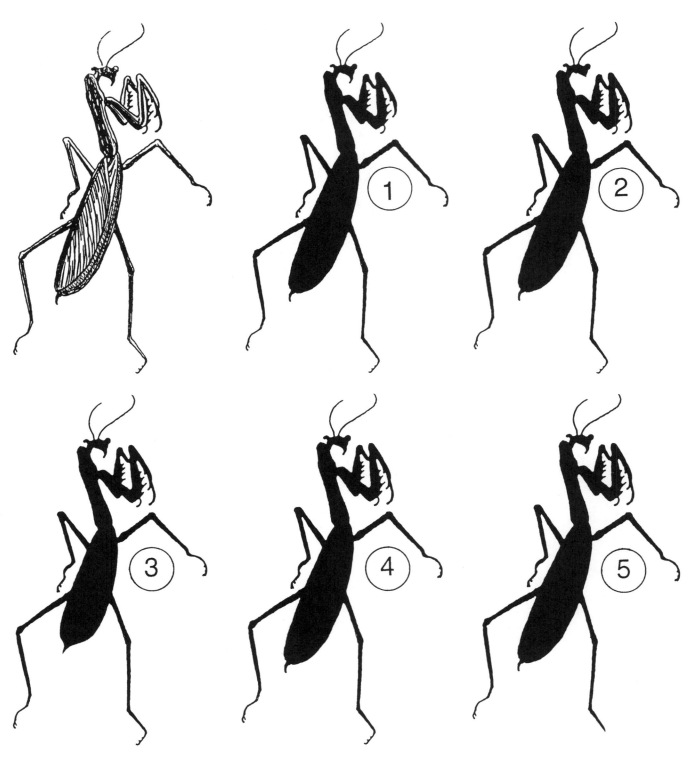

Answer: Shadow number four.

Try drawing the other half of this Atlantic lobster. If you like your lobster cooked, color it red; if not, color it grey-brown.

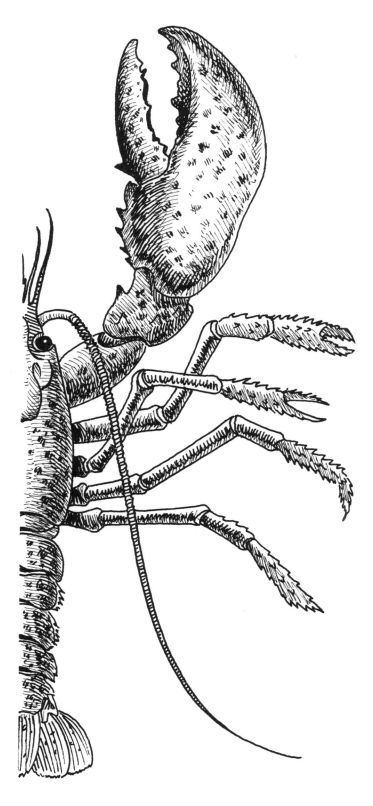

The cougar, or mountain lion, is seldom seen. See if you can find one hiding in the space below by filling in all the even-numbered shapes.

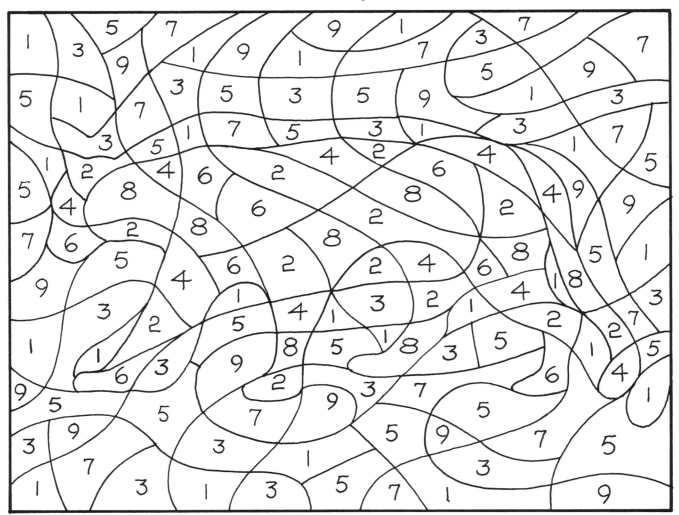

NATURE NOTES

The bobcat is smaller and more reddish in color than its cousin, the Canada lynx. Since most of its hunting is done at dusk, it is not often seen.

Butterflies, like all insects, have six legs. Seven insects are hiding in the square below. Find them by looking across or down.

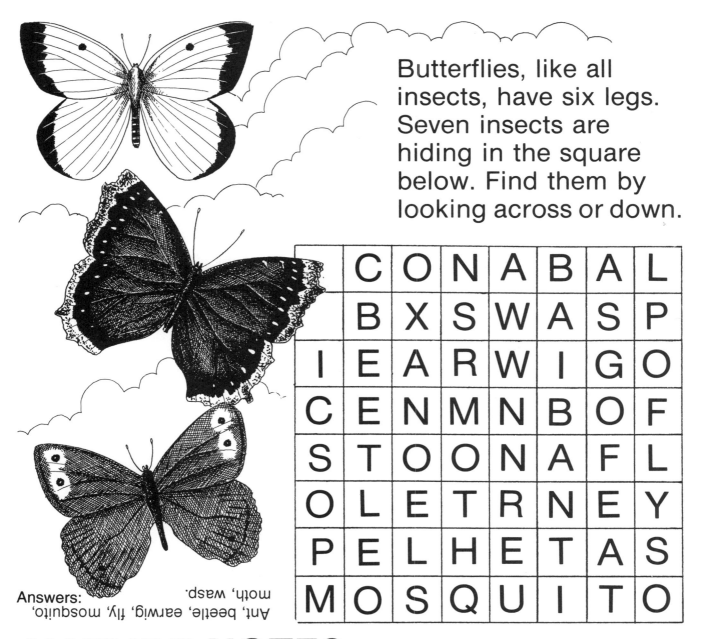

C	O	N	A	B	A	L
B	X	S	W	A	S	P
I	E	A	R	W	I	G	O
C	E	N	M	N	B	O	F
S	T	O	O	N	A	F	L
O	L	E	T	R	N	E	Y
P	E	L	H	E	T	A	S
M	O	S	Q	U	I	T	O

NATURE NOTES

The cabbage butterfly is a common pest that came to North America in 1868 and in only 20 years spread over the entire continent.

Here are two pictures of a pair of snowy owls.
Try to find six things that are different in picture two.

Answers:

1: Feet missing on owl at right.
2: Nail missing on fence rail.
3: Spots missing on head of owl at left.
4: Beak missing on owl at left.
5: Snow on fence rail missing.
6: Clouds at right are missing.

To find out which animal left these tracks just unscramble the letters.

1 FRONT HIND
GERDAB

2 FRONT HIND
LFWO

3 FRONT HIND
NIPPORUCE

4 FRONT HIND
EVRABE

5 FRONT HIND
COCARON

6 FRONT HIND
KNUKS

7 FRONT HIND
SOPSUMO

8 FRONT HIND
ECTOYO

9 FRONT HIND
YXNL

Answers:
1.Badger 2.Wolf 3.Porcupine 4.Beaver 5.Raccoon 6.Skunk 7.Opossum 8.Coyote 9.Lynx

One letter, when added to the letters in each of the six sections, will help spell out the names of six desert dwellers. Place that letter in the inner circle.

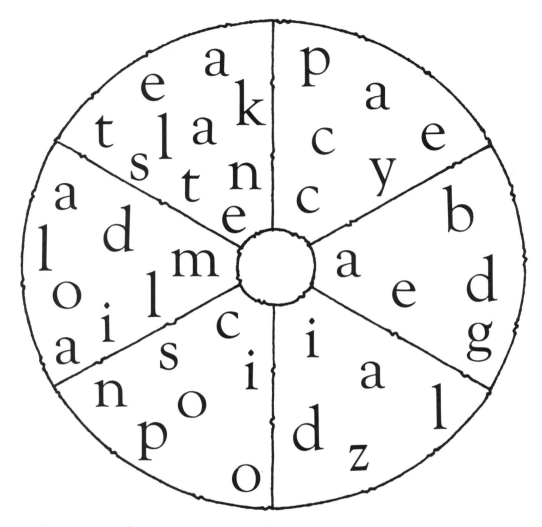

DID YOU KNOW?

The horned toad is not a toad, but a lizard. When frightened, this lizard may squirt a stream of blood from the corners of its eyes.

Which shadow belongs to this painted turtle?

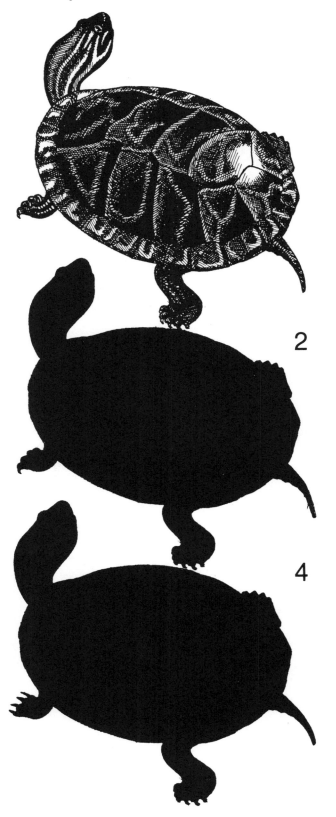

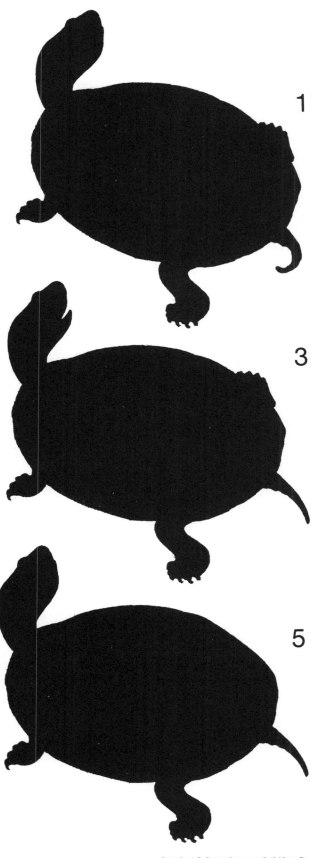

1

2

3

4

5

Answer: Shadow number two

How many snakes can you count on this page?

Answer: There are nineteen snakes.

The jaguar, once native to the southwestern United States, was hunted to extinction in the U.S. It is now rare in Mexico and Central America. A large jaguar may measure almost eight feet from nose to tip of tail. See how well you can draw the other half of this jaguar's head.

This picture of a rainbow trout has been drawn with one continuous line. See if you can find the end of the line.

When you have found the end of the line, color the trout and put speckles on it.

START HERE →

To find out what this waterfowl's name is, start at the "H" and read every second letter. Go around twice.

Answer: Hooded merganser.

Pelicans usually travel in flocks. Can you count the number of pelicans in this flock?

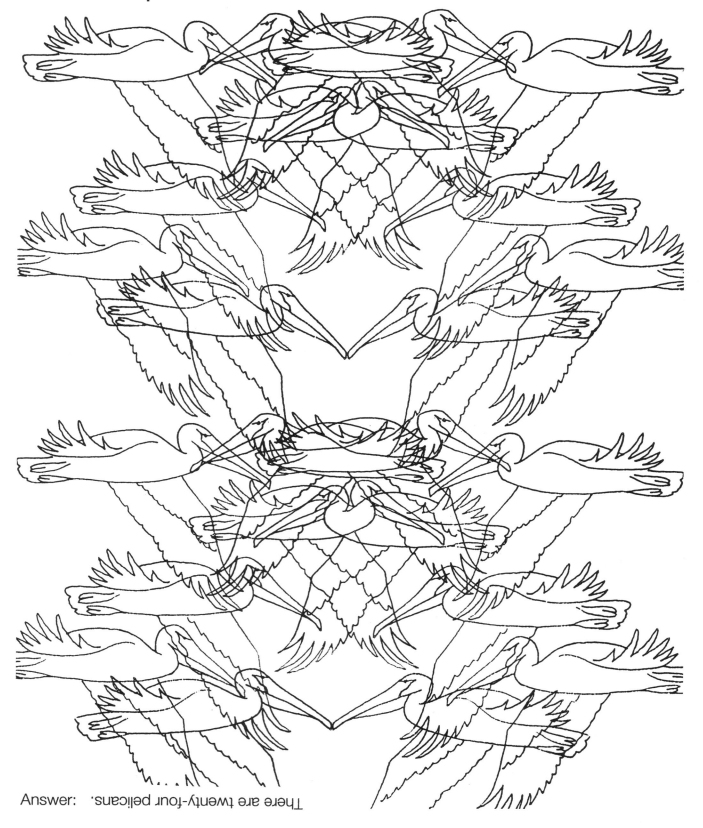

Answer: There are twenty-four pelicans.

Mammals feed their young with milk. Which of the creatures shown below are mammals? Draw a line under the names of those you think are mammals.

Killer Whale

Cowbird

Crab

Sea Lion

Butterfly

Bat

Rattlesnake

Starfish

Frog

Rabbit

River Otter

Basking Shark

Answers: Killer whale, sea lion, bat, river otter, rabbit.

The tarpon, found in the Gulf of Mexico, may grow to eight feet in length and weigh 250 pounds. Try copying this one in the squares below.

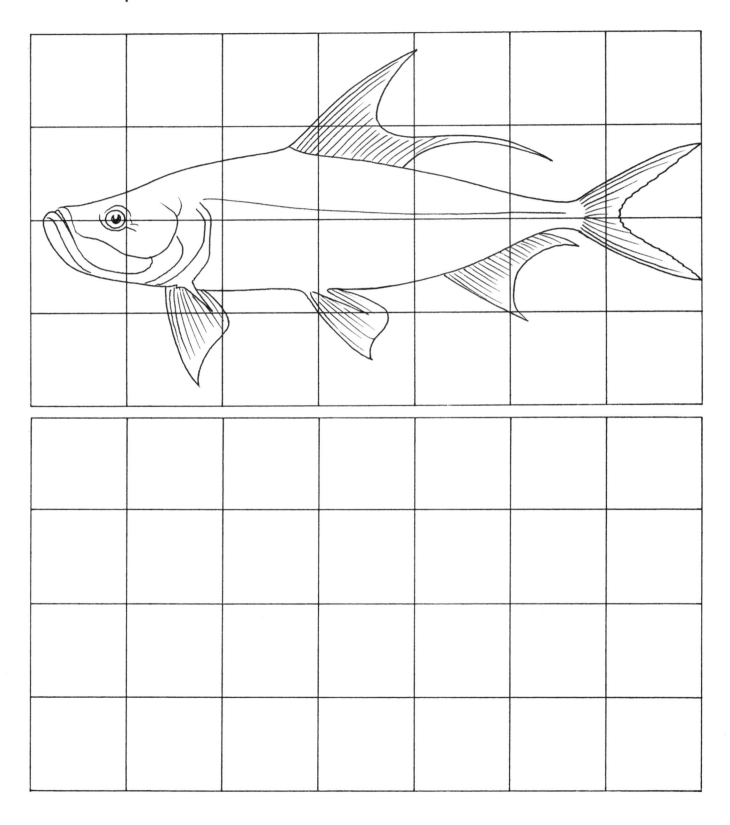

The wild turkey is a poor flyer but a fast runner. How many three-letter words can you make from the letters in the words "wild turkey"?
Try for twenty-seven.

WILD TURKEY

_____

_____

_____

_____

_____

_____

Copy the black parts of these squares into the square below with the same number. You will create a good picture of something you wouldn't want to meet.

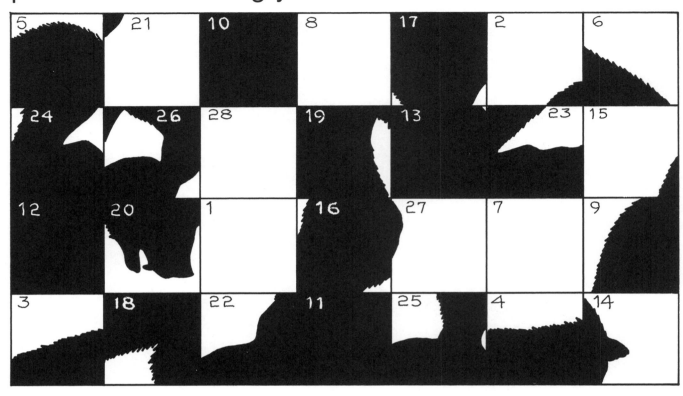

1	2	3	4	5	6	7
8	9	10	11	12	13	14
15	16	17	18	19	20	21
22	23	24	25	26	27	28

Fill in the squares with letters that spell the names of the creatures shown on this page.

The caracara, or Mexican eagle, is the national emblem of Mexico. Which two of these birds are identical?

The insects shown here may be seen flying over ponds or slow-moving streams. To find what their names are, just unscramble the letters.

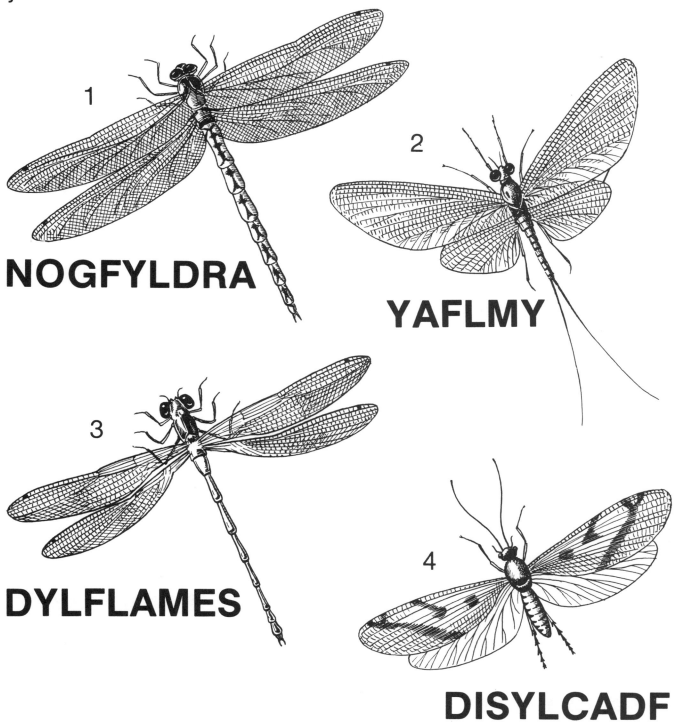

1 **NOGFYLDRA**

2 **YAFLMY**

3 **DYLFLAMES**

4 **DISYLCADF**

Answers: 1. Dragonfly 2. Mayfly 3. Damselfly 4. Caddisfly

This woodchuck, or groundhog, has dug itself into a deep hole. Can you help it out?

Here are two pictures of a collared lizard.
Can you find six things different in picture two?

Which shadow belongs to the peregrine falcon?

Answer: Shadow number one.

Here are two pictures of a brook trout. Can you find six things that are different in picture number two?

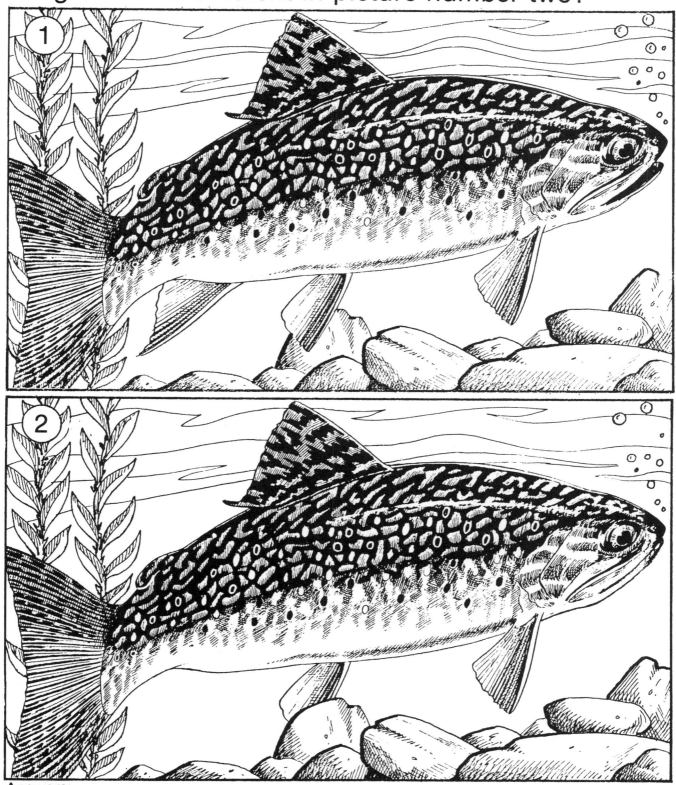

Answers:

1: Trout's mouth is closed. 2: Fin near tail is missing. 3: Second water line from top is missing. 4: One bubble is missing. 5: The fin is behind the rock at center of picture. 6: Leaf is missing from plant behind trout's tail.

Search across and down in this giant puzzle to find thirteen forest dwellers.

L O B A T E N Z O L E P
R U B L U E J A Y E L A
A C H O C O L A T E K E
B C A B D C E B E A R E
W O L V E R I N E O M S
O U P I E C A K R H A T
G A K R Q C O Y O T E
B A D G E R X L L R E M
A R M O S T R A L N L B
D O B E A V E R O E S E
P R E S E N I T S T A E
A D R A G O N F L Y

Try your hand at drawing the other half of this beautiful swallowtail butterfly. Then color it yellow.

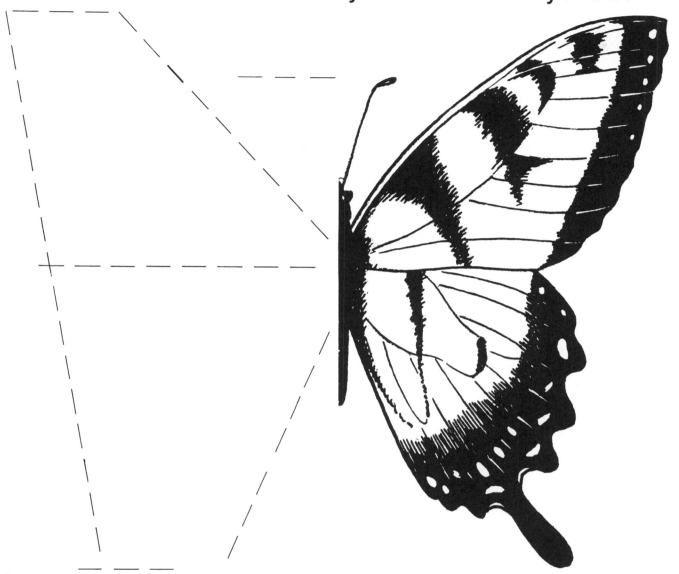

DID YOU KNOW?

Flying squirrels don't really fly. They glide by means of a membrane that stretches from front to back legs.

The letters surrounding this marlin have been strung together to spell the names of ten sea dwellers. Can you find them?

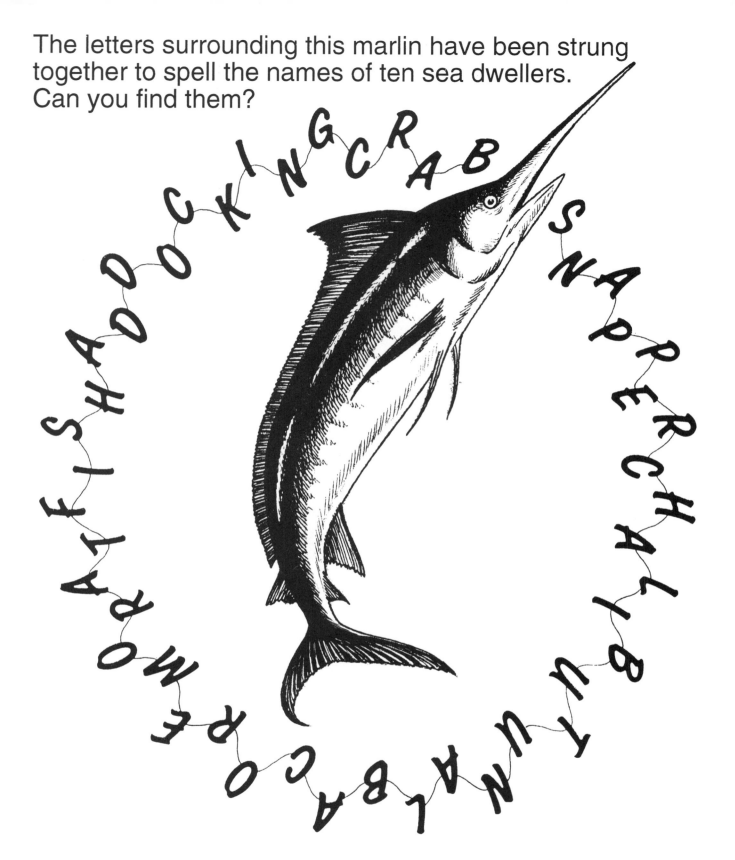

Can you separate the geese from the foxes by drawing only four straight lines?

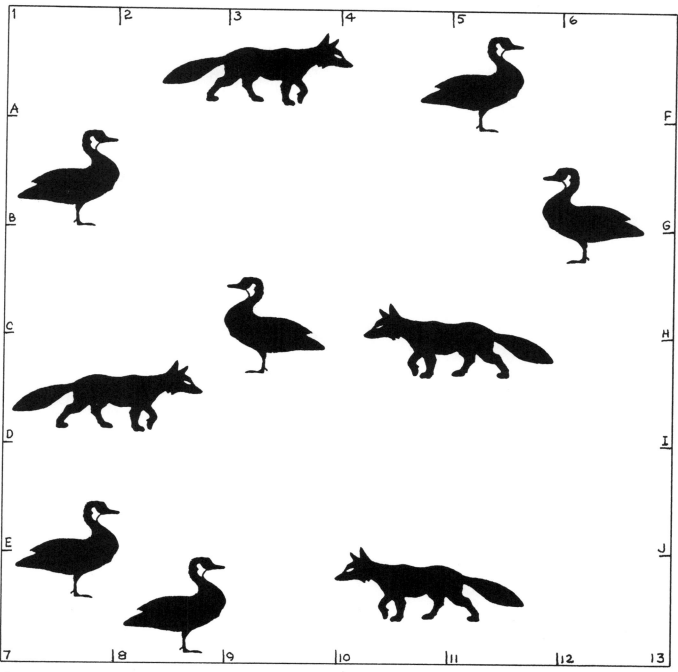

Answer: Draw straight lines from D to 11, B to 13, 1 to 13, and 4 to 1

This little resident of the southwestern United States and Mexico is a relative of the raccoon. To find out what its name is, trace the line from letter to letter, spelling as you go.

Answer: It is called a ringtail cat even though it is not really a cat.

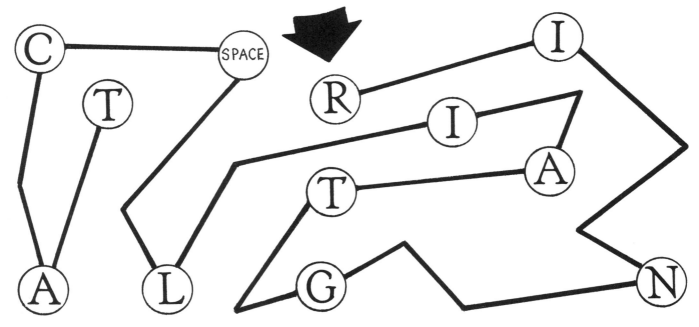

This noisy little duck may be found on both our coasts. To find this duck's name, fill in the blank above each letter with the letter that appears before it in the alphabet.

$\overline{~~}$ C $\overline{~~}$ B $\overline{~~}$ S $\overline{~~}$ S $\overline{~~}$ P $\overline{~~}$ X'T

$\overline{~~}$ H $\overline{~~}$ P $\overline{~~}$ M $\overline{~~}$ E $\overline{~~}$ F $\overline{~~}$ O $\overline{~~}$ F $\overline{~~}$ Z $\overline{~~}$ F

DID YOU KNOW?

There are more than forty-five species of swans, ducks, and geese that are native to North America.

Try to make as many words
as you can from the letters
in the word "wildlife."
There are more than sixteen.

WILDLIFE

Answer: Albacore number five

Which shadow belongs to the kangaroo rat?

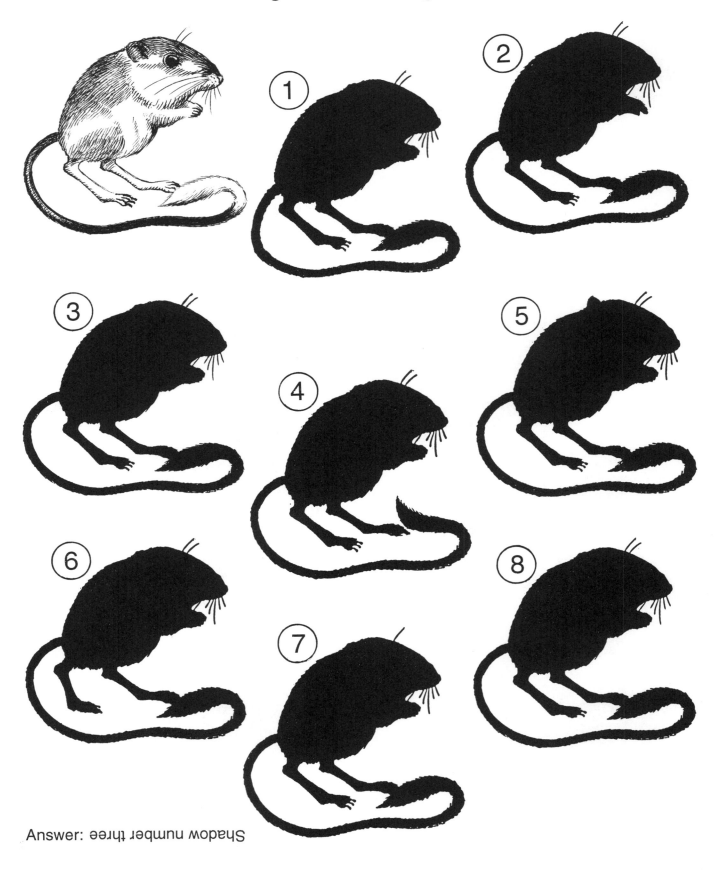

Answer: Shadow number three

Here is a secret code to study. Now try to read the very important message below.

When you can read the message, make up some of your own. Try them on your friends.

Here are two pictures of a pair of beavers.
Try to find six things different in picture two.

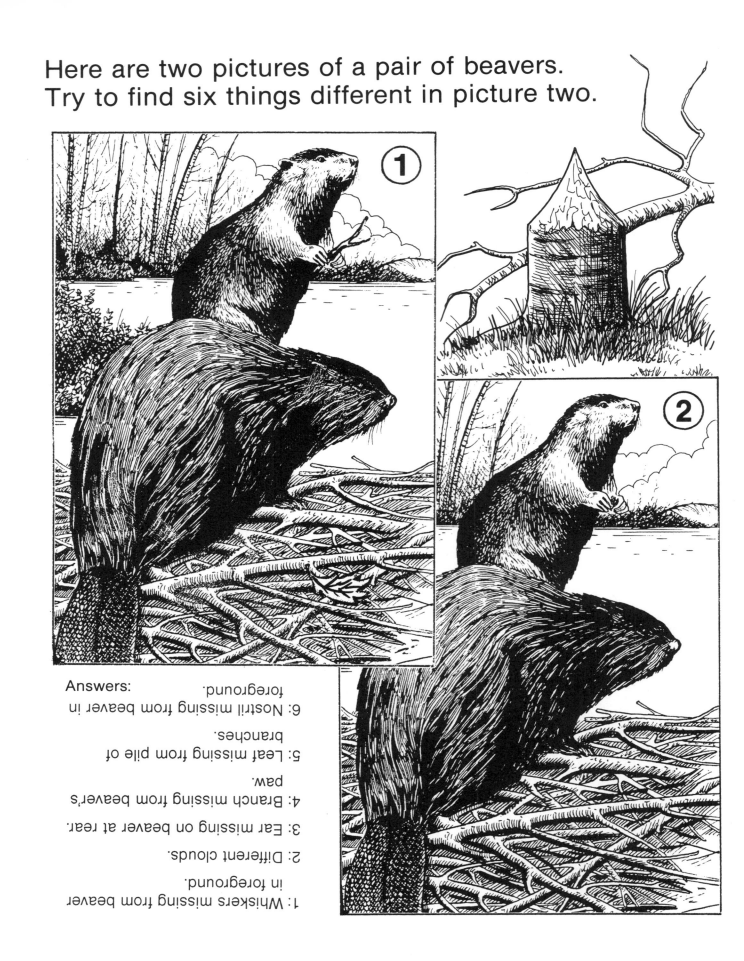

Answers:

1: Whiskers missing from beaver in foreground.

2: Different clouds.

3: Ear missing on beaver at rear.

4: Branch missing from beaver's paw.

5: Leaf missing from pile of branches.

6: Nostril missing from beaver in foreground.

Several species of dolphin inhabit the waters surrounding
North America. Try drawing these, one square at a time.

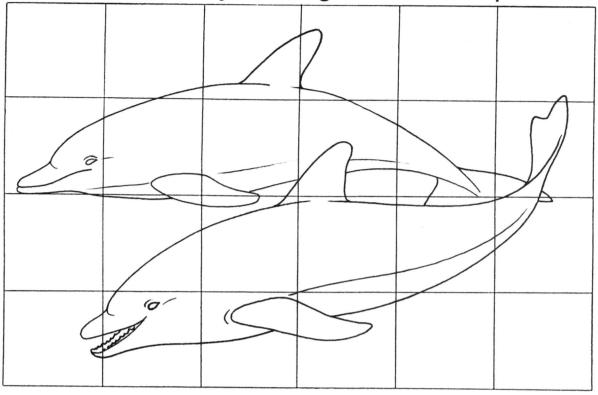

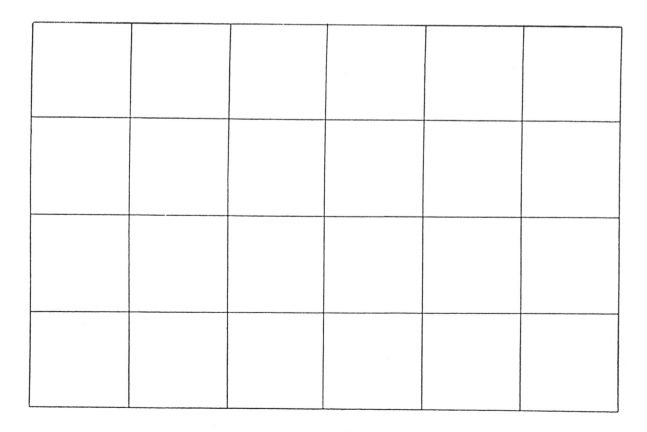

To find the names of these birds, follow the line, spelling as you go.

Animals that eat meat are called carnivores, while animals that eat vegetation are called herbivores, and animals that eat just about anything are called omnivores. Decide which animals below are carnivore, herbivore, or omnivore and print the appropriate name in each rectangle.

Four children hope to catch this small-mouth bass.
Follow their fishing lines to see which bait it is about
to take.

Kevin   Linda   Steve   Erin

Find the letters missing from the alphabet in each box, then rearrange them to spell the name of the shore bird in the box.

Box 1:
a w h m j
l y r b
u v z g
f x t o q
c k d

Box 2:
f n p k
o v x j
h y t d
q z m
b i s g a

Box 3:
c k u d
g y z j a
s f q m
h w x
n t i b

Since this marmot doesn't want to become some other animal's dinner, it is worried about what it sees on the ridge behind it. If you fill in all the triangle shapes with your pencil or crayon, you will see what the marmot is afraid of.

Can you find the shadow that belongs to this hornet?

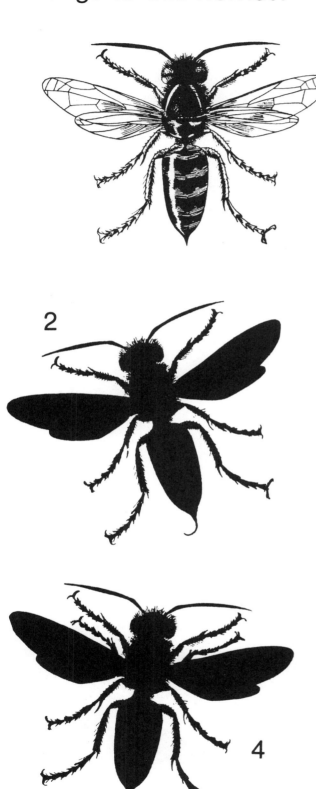

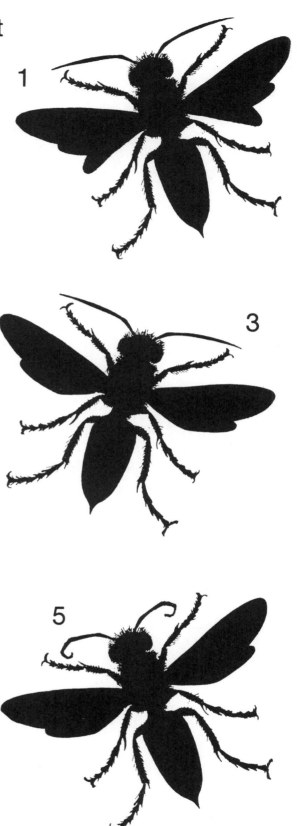

How well can you draw the missing halves of the two salmon below?

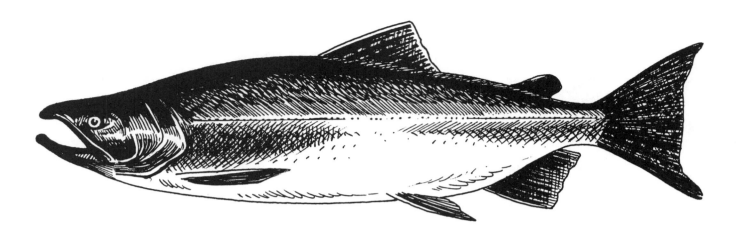

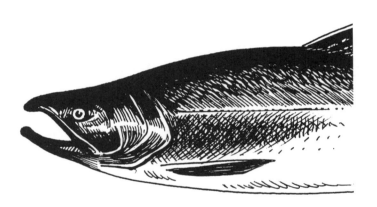

CHICKADEE

How many words can you make from the letters in my name? There are at least ten.

_____   _____

_____   _____

_____   _____

_____   _____

_____   _____

_____   _____

Answer: Ace, cad, check, chick, deck, die, each, eke, had, head, heed, hide, idea

These four picture puzzles contain the names of four different mammals.

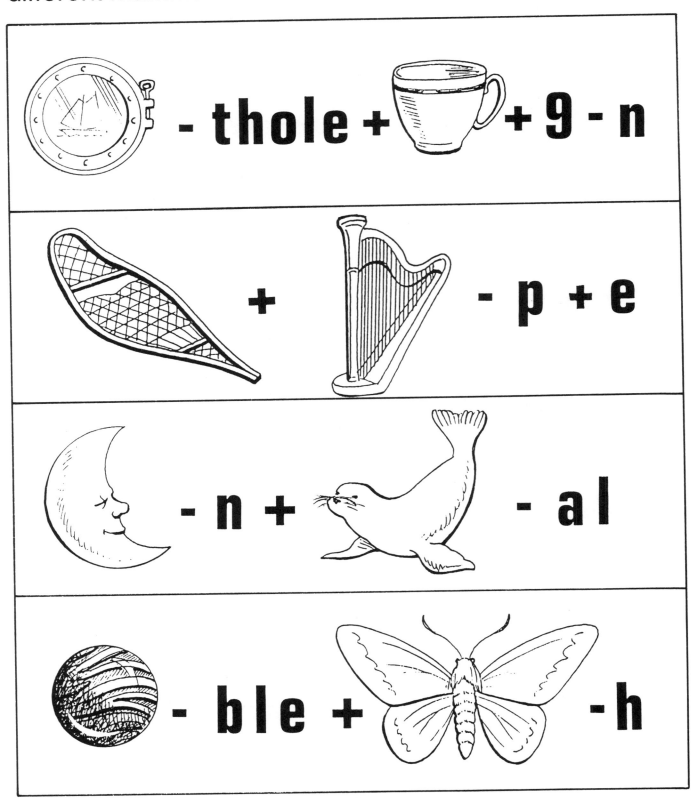

Twelve birds are hiding in the letters surrounding these bobwhite quail. See if you can find them.

KILLDEERGOOSEAGULLARKINGFISHERONUTHATCHICKADEEAGLEGRETERNIGHTHAWK

Here are two pictures of a grizzly bear.
Can you find six things different in picture two?

Answers: 1: Tree missing at left. 2: Point missing on sheep's horn. 3: Rock missing at right. 4: Bear's left front leg missing. 5: Bear's ear missing. 6: Branch different.

Copy the black parts of each square into the square below with the same number. If it's done carefully, a picture of a mother and her baby will appear.

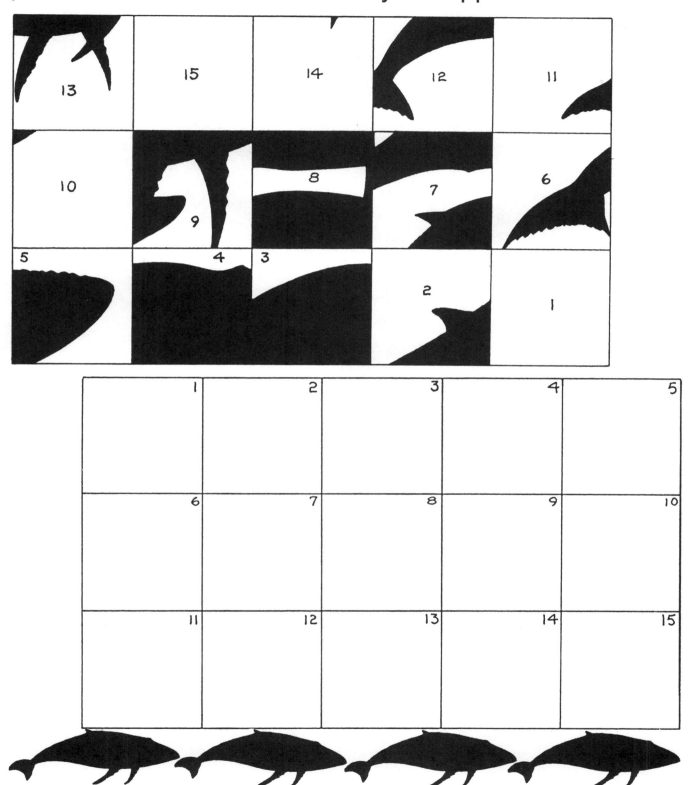

Which shadow belongs to this whitetail deer?

1

2

3

4

Answer: Shadow number three

Ten animals are hiding in the sentences below. Can you find them?

1. It is not good enough to be average.
2. Kelly gave Omar ten bananas.
3. Wampum and beads were traded.
4. Try to be artistic when you draw.
5. Bad germs should be washed away.
6. Wade erased the chalkboard.
7. Muriel knows how to swim.
8. Randy and Karen never ate candy.
9. The weather got terribly cold.
10. Lindsay and Josh are brothers.

This armor-plated armadillo uses its long, sticky tongue to catch insects, its main source of food. See how many three-letter words you can make with the letters in the word "armadillo."

ARMADILLO

_____

_____

_____

_____

_____

NAME THE WEASELS...

From the information below, you can figure out the names of these weasels. Print their names in the rectangles beneath them.

- Wesley is beneath Willy.
- Willy is above Wally.
- Wesley is not in the middle.

This drawing of a bald eagle has been completed with one continuous line. See if you can find the end of the line.

START HERE

These two fish are cousins and very popular with fresh-water anglers. To find their names, over each letter write the letter that comes before it in the alphabet.

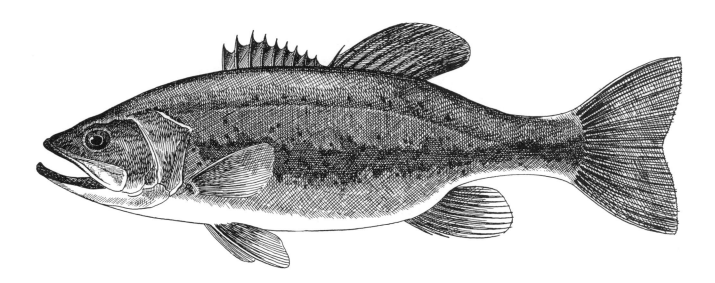

M B S H F N P V U I   C B T T

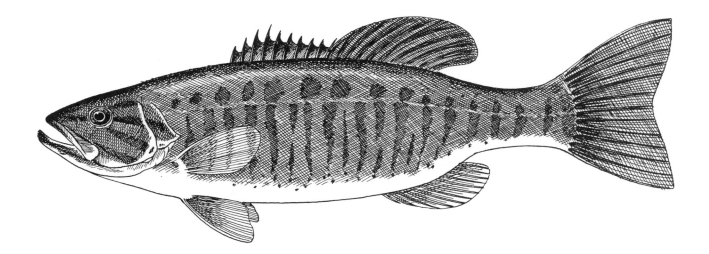

T N B M M N P V U I   C B T T

While these two little sandpipers search the shore for seafood morsels, twelve other shore birds are hiding in the squares below. Search for them by looking across or down.

B	L	T	X	P	O	N	T	G	O	D	W	I	T	K
X	D	U	N	L	I	N	Z	O	G	H	I	M	N	I
A	V	O	L	O	A	C	G	S	T	I	L	T	X	L
V	D	N	E	V	B	D	H	K	N	Q	L	T	Y	L
O	Y	S	T	E	R	C	A	T	C	H	E	R	Z	D
C	A	N	E	R	K	E	I	L	O	R	T	U	A	E
E	S	I	S	A	N	D	E	R	L	I	N	G	B	E
T	I	P	M	Q	O	F	J	M	P	S	V	W	C	R
R	J	E	N	P	T	U	R	N	S	T	O	N	E	P

Answers:
Avocet, dunlin, godwit, killdeer, knot, oyster catcher, plover, sanderling, snipe, stilt, turnstone, willet.

The wolf may weigh more than 65 kilograms.
Try drawing this one by copying one square
at a time.

Find the names of these three North American game birds by unscrambling the letters next to them.

LAFINCOARI AUQLI

NIATUNOM LIQUA

WOBITHEB ULAIQ

Help this little pika through the rock slide to the grass it has cut and dried for winter food.

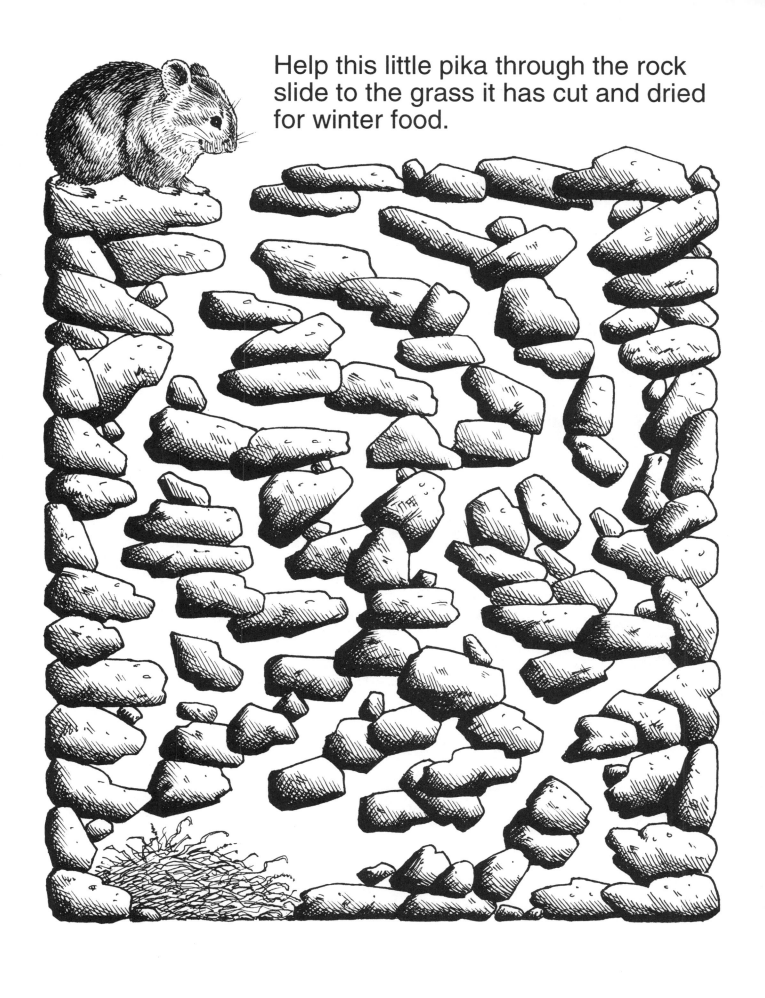

This school of cod contains three sets of twins. Can you pick them out?

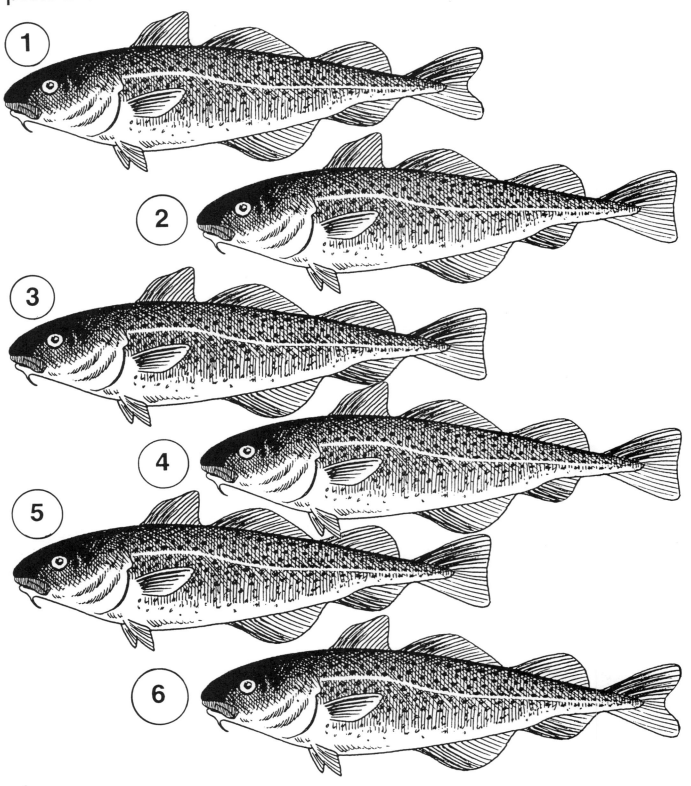

Answers:
Cods numbered one and six. Cods numbered two and four. Cods numbered three and five.

Find this little cottontail's brother by filling in all the shapes having odd numbers.

To find this bird's name, start at the letter "E" and read every second letter. Go around twice. The name consists of two words.

The gray, or timber, wolf was once common throughout
North America. It is now found only in the remote
areas of Canada and Alaska. See how well you can draw
the other half of this wolf's head.

Can you separate the mice from the rattlesnakes by drawing only four straight lines?

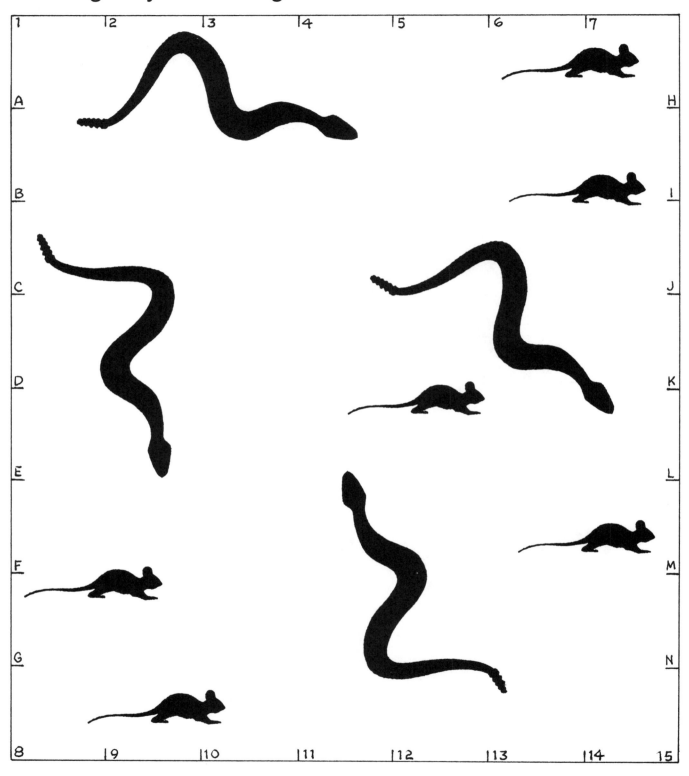

Answer: Draw straight lines from C to 11, A to 15, A to L, and 4 to K.

Hi there! It's me again. Remember, the spelling bee? This time I want you to decide which of the animal names below are spelled correctly.

snowshoe hair	snowshoe hare
wale	whale
muscrat	muskrat
mule deer	mule dear
mole	moal
weasel	weezle
porcupine	porkupine
beever	beaver
walrus	whalrus
Arctic fox	Artic fox
wolvereen	wolverine

Have someone time you while you study the creatures on this page for one minute. Then close the book and write down the names of all the creatures you remember. Twelve would be good. Sixteen would be great!

CANADA GOOSE

RABBIT

BISON

SALMON

PHEASANT

CHICKADEE

HERRING

SALAMANDER

HORNWORM

OWL

MOUSE

QUAIL

FROG

PERCH

CURLEW

SNOW GOOSE

Here are eight ringneck
pheasants. They are all
different except for two.
Try to find the twins.

Answer: Pheasants three and six

THE AUTHOR

Tom Hunter is a respected wildlife artist who resides outside Vancouver, B.C. Over the past twelve years Tom has developed a series of wildlife activity books featuring primarily fishes, birds, insects, and various four-legged creatures found in Canada and the northern United States.

Published under the titles *Canadian Wildlife Activity Books* (Volume One, Two, and Three) these thoughtful collections have entertained children, parents, and teachers alike. *Critters for Kids* combines many of Tom's choices from earlier books with new work that emphasises animals of the south—from the armadillo to the scorpion.

Tom Hunter's books have won wide acclaim both for the quality of his artwork and the educational value of the material. More copies of this book and those illustrated below may be ordered through your local bookseller or by mail order.

Canadian Wildlife Activity Book
Volume 1 • ISBN 0-919214-55-X • $7.95
Volume 2 • ISBN 0-919214-83-5 • $7.95
Volume 3 • ISBN 1-895811-66-X • $8.95

Mail orders should include $4.00 plus $1.00 per book for postage and handling. Send orders to
Heritage House Publishing Co. Ltd., #108 - 17665 - 66 A Avenue, Surrey, B.C. Canada V3S 2A7